Count With Me

CRYSTAL SIKKENS

HOW HEAVY?

A Crabtree Roots Book

Crabtree Publishing
crabtreebooks.com

School-to-Home Support for Caregivers and Teachers

This book helps children grow by letting them practice reading. Here are a few guiding questions to help the reader with building his or her comprehension skills. Possible answers appear here in red.

Before Reading:

- What do I think this book is about?
    - *I think this book is about things that are heavy and things that are light.*
    - *I think this book is about measuring how heavy something is.*

- What do I want to learn about this topic?
    - *I want to learn what weight is.*
    - *I want to learn what I can use to find out how heavy something is.*

During Reading:

- I wonder why...
    - *I wonder why some things are light and some are heavy.*
    - *I wonder why there are different kinds of scales.*

- What have I learned so far?
    - *I have learned that weight is how heavy something is.*
    - *I have learned that a rock is heavy and a feather is light.*

After Reading:

- What details did I learn about this topic?
    - *I have learned that some scales can be used to measure how heavy something is.*
    - *I have learned that when one side of a scale goes down, the object is heavier.*

- Read the book again and look for the vocabulary words.
    - *I see the word **weight** on page 3 and the word **heavy** on page 4. The other vocabulary words are found on page 14.*

I want to learn about **weight**.

Weight is how heavy something is. This rock is **heavy**.

Feathers are **light**.

I can use a **scale** to find out how heavy something is.

Some scales show which object is heavier.

The watermelon goes down. It is heavier.

Word List

Sight Words

a	find	it	to
about	goes	out	use
are	how	some	want
can	I	the	which
down	is	this	

Words to Know

heavy

light

scale

weight

45 Words

I want to learn about **weight**.

Weight is how heavy something is. This rock is **heavy**.

Feathers are **light**.

I can use a **scale** to find out how heavy something is.

Some scales show which object is heavier.

The watermelon goes down. It is heavier.

Count With Me

HOW HEAVY?

Crabtree Publishing

crabtreebooks.com 800-387-7650

 In Canada: We acknowledge the financial support of the Government of Canada through the Canada Book Fund for our publishing activities.

Hardcover 978-1-0398-7268-4
Paperback 978-1-0398-7326-1
Ebook (pdf) 978-1-0398-7383-4
Epub 978-1-0398-7432-9

Published in Canada
Crabtree Publishing
616 Welland Avenue
St. Catharines, Ontario
L2M 5V6

Published in the United States
Crabtree Publishing
347 Fifth Avenue
Suite 1402-145
New York, NY 10016

Written by: Crystal Sikkens
Designed by: Margaret Salter
Proofreader: Kathy Middleton
Photographs: Shutterstock.com
Production manager: Candice Campbell

Printed in the U.S.A./CP022026